Follow The
Light

Finding Hope in A Dark Place

Tasha Paige

Just a Voice Media

Finding Hope in A Dark Place

Tasha Paige

Just a Voice Media

Contents

Follow the Light 6
Day 1 8
Day 2 9
Day 3 10
Day 4 11
Day 5 12
Day 6 13
Day 7 14
Day 8 15
Day 9 16
Day 10 17
Day 11 19
Day 12 20
Day 13 21
Day 14 22
Day 15 23
Day 16 24
Day 17 25
Day 18 26
Day 19 27
Day 20 28

Day 21 30

Day 22 31

Day 23 32

Day 24 33

Day 25 34

Day 26 35

Day 27 36

Day 28 37

Day 29 38

Day 30 39

Day 31 41

Day 32 42

Day 33 43

Day 34 44

Day 35 45

Day 36 46

Day 37 47

Day 38 48

Day 39 49

Day 40 50

Day 41 52

Day 42 53

Day 43 54

Day 44 55

Day 45 56

Day 46 57

Day 47 58

Day 48 59

Day 49 60

Day 50 62

Day 51 64

Day 52 65

Day 53 66

Day 54 67

Day 55 68

Day 56 70

Day 57 72

Day 58 73

Day 59 74

DAY 60 76

Follow the Light

Daily Inspirations from the book of Psalms

After eight years of walking with God, I had no idea of where God's providence would take me and open up my spirit to receive His Word. What you are about to read are the very words God breathed inside of me from day to day, then from weekend to weekend as I sat in jail.

God walked with me as I was moved out of a church building into a place where I became the church. The Lord revealed to me how many of His precious jewels are missing; only waiting for God's ambassadors to unlock their beauty.

These daily inspirations from the Lord are what my God gave me to share with my incarcerated sisters; in return, the Lord drew them to the cross, and revealed His illuminating love in a dark period of their lives. Take a deep breath, close your eyes and ask God to let these words sink into your Spirit.

Walk with me as I walked with God in a time that appeared to be my darkest moment ever, and yet as promised the light did **Shine.**

Arise, shine; for thy light is come, and the glory of the Lord is risen upon thee. Isaiah 60:1

Day 1

I will sing of your love and justice; to you, O Lord, I will sing Praise.

Psalm 101:1

In times of darkness, praise alone brings the Son's shine. No artificial light will take you to the height of praise. Getting involved with the pleasures of the world's system will only intoxicate you into thinking that sin brings illumination. During these times, true praise draws God to you and in you. It was during those moments that I had to push myself to praise, so that I could stay close to God. These seasons will birth freshness in the spirit or freshness in the flesh. It must be your choice to decide which way you want to go; higher in God or lower in the devil. True praise must be tested before it is allowed to be given in the presence of the Almighty because true praise is not just an act or emotion but a lifestyle we live no matter the circumstances of our lives. Sometimes the love and justice of God does not unfold the way we desire, and it's in those very moments when we must trust that God is moving in a way that is best for us.

Lord, give me the strength to praise you when things seem to be at their worst. I yoke up with you during this trial, knowing and believing in your Word that all things are working together for my good. Thank you, God, for victory. In the name of Jesus, Amen

Day 2

In the beginning you laid the foundations of the earth, and the heavens are the work of your hands. They will perish, but you remain; they will all wear out like a garment. But you remain the same, and your years will never end.

Psalm 102:5, 26a, 27

God never changes, nor will He ever change. Without accepting Jesus Christ as our Savior and letting Him reign as Lord, everything that is created by God will eventually perish. God must see a reflection of His Son in us in order to be translated from mortal to immortal. For mankind to taste of this pleasure, God's sign must be visible to His penetrating eye. God is searching us for more than an outward appearance of Christ; God is looking within. Public expressions are evidence to people that you serve God but God seeks for evidence in secret. In order to enter into the promised eternal life, God must see His Son operating towards Him and man in its true origin. God has put an expiration date on all things earthly; that's why He sent His Son Jesus with a way of escape from the destruction. God has no desire for us to perish but wants us to accept His plan so we too may live an eternal life with Him.

Lord, I realize that this life will pass away but eternal life has no end. Father, I want to live with you in that eternity. I accept Christ Jesus as your Son and my Savior; I repent of my sins and turn from the world's allurements. Give me an appetite for your pleasures. Thank you, God, for victory. In the name of Jesus, Amen.

Day 3

Praise the Lord, O my soul, and forget not all His benefits. He does not treat us as our sins deserve, or repay us according to our iniquities.

Psalm 103:2, 10

In our times of affliction, God's grace is still a shield from the true blow administered by the enemy. As we go through painful circumstances, if we stay focused on the fact that He has compassion for us, it will thrust our innermost parts to praise His name; which means to praise His character. God will not allow us to go through more than we are able to bear, He will sustain us through the floods of suffering. The choices that I made brought such pain in my life but even then God was there to help distribute the blow so that it would not kill me. Oftentimes we look for God's quick deliverance from these situations, but God gives us strength to go through and see sin in its real destructing form. We deserved greater repayment for our acts of sin, but our God is more merciful than we give Him credit for.

Lord, I feel as though I am drowning in my pain. My tears wet my pillow night after night. Lord, rise up during this time of affliction and save me. Father, it seems as if night has come and I can't see my way. Lead me safely to the other side. Lord, thank you for your merciful ways that are evident in your dealings with me. In Jesus' name, Amen.

Day 4

He waters the mountains from His upper chamber; the earth is satisfied by the fruit of His work.

Psalm 104:13

God's creative power is the glue that holds the worlds together. God created with order and beauty. God framed a world that would obey His power in all of mankind. God created with the thought that He wanted man to be His delight, so He satisfied the delight of man. God is never too far that He cannot maintain the order of everything that He has created. There has never been too much chaos going on in my life that God was not able to have control over. The problem was that I did not give God the authority to have control, nor did I operate in the authority He had given me to keep control. God will allow things to get out of control so that we may truly see how helpless we are against the vices of the enemy. I had to learn, my friends, that sometimes God has to allow my pieces to fall apart so His can come together in my life.

Father, help me to realize that when you are allowed to have to have control things function at their best. Though things seem to be in an uproar all around me, God, you are not stressed about the outcome. Lord, help me to trust in your authority and rest in your power. In Jesus' name, Amen.

Day 5

Joseph remained a slave until his own words had come true and the Lord had finished testing him.

Psalm 105:19

Even though you may have physical chains on you, spiritually you can be free. Slavery only sets you up for promotion when you hold fast to what God has revealed to you. Slavery is a testing ground to become a leader for the Kingdom of God. The Lord has a set date on which the trial you are going through will end, hold fast because promotion is on the way. Only those whom God can test will be the ones He will trust to elevate. Before the Hebrew boys went into a fire that was seven times hotter, they had been in other fires to prepare them for this one. The best way to handle heat is to be put in it time and time again. Each degree higher the fire is, that is another level in promotion. God must know that the things I am asking Him to do for me will be accomplished for His glory, so I must be tested. I have come to realize that, many times, what we are going through is not just for us but for those we will be able to help through at a later time in life.

Lord, though I feel bound I know that things aren't always as they seem. Help me, Lord, to see beyond the physical and hold on to the promises that you have spoken to me. Lord, I am weak and I admit this, but your Word says these are the times that I become strong. I call upon that strength in Jesus' name I pray, Amen.

Day 6

No one can praise you enough for all the mighty things you have done.

Psalm 106:2

When can we come to the place where praising God is excessive? When we pay honor to our false gods we never tire of praising. We are at a point in Christianity where we only praise with our intelligence, but God is calling us back to a place where we give all we have to Him, with no restrictions or limitations simply because of who He is and who He wants to be in our lives. We often praise when we want some financial blessing or we need God to bail us out of trouble, so we make all these empty promises to Him. God is going to become deaf to this fake, self-driven praise because He is seeking true worship in spirit and in truth. I believe we must come to a place in our situations where, no matter the outcome, God deserves my praise. In the Bible, from Genesis to Revelation, we find God being praised from the lips of the writers, from those He healed, and even creation is noted for praising God, and even with all that praise there is still more to give. May we join in on this great praise chorus and exalt our Great God.

God, may I never tire in praising your Holy name. Lord, help me to realize that, if I tire here on Earth to praise you, then I will be unfit for heaven where the very atmosphere is praise. Lord, may my lips be saturated with your praises. In Jesus' name, Amen.

Day 7

You should praise the Lord for His love and for the wonderful things he does for all of us.

Psalm 107:31

Everyone at some point in life has been tossed around by personal storms of pain. We have been roaming the earth, being guided by our own lust. We have set ourselves up as gods, thinking we can heal, prosper, and lead ourselves into peace. What we give ourselves is temporal and very sorrowful to our spirits. Sins keep us bound but God is ever waiting for us to call unto Him for help, so He may deliver and strengthen us to walk in obedience. The human race is indebted to God. The evidence of His wonder is all around us and we should live to honor Him. I could never see the evidence while I was drunk on the devil's lies. True praise opens up the mind to receive the unadulterated truth from God.

Father God, I have been so consumed in my pain that I have not acknowledged the wonders you have wrought in my life. Lord, help me to focus on you and to praise you through every storm. In Jesus' name, Amen.

Day 8

Be exalted, O God, above the heavens, and let your glory be over all the earth.

Psalm 108:5

God accepts us as we are, how we are, but He desires us to grow in grace. As a babe in Christ, you won't experience the fullness of His love because you can't grasp the depth of how real love operates. You must grow in order to become better equipped in the Word and the love of God. This growth helps us better understand the authority that God has given to us through His Son. Through this growth, people will see God's glory arising in our lives and will inquire of you about this change. God's only place in our lives is to be first, and our duty is to exalt Him in that place. Exaltation will require total abandonment to God and all other idols must be put away. The Lord wants to sit on the throne of our hearts; He doesn't just want to be our Savior, He wants to be Lord of our lives.

Father, even when I was a sinner you accepted me as I was. You withheld no love to bring me closer to you. Lord, help me not to withhold from you what you rightfully deserve. In Jesus' name, Amen.

Day 9

Help me, O Lord my God; save me in accordance with your love.

Psalm 109:26

Salvation comes through love. God does what He does for us based on His love not according to a feeling that He gets. It is His principle; it's who He is. AGAPE love breaks all barriers of emotionalism. The principle of love will keep you grounded in the Word much longer than an emotion. God needs some followers that can go the distance whether or not they feel like it. Perfect love knows the truth about God in and out of every season. The very reason love exists is because God does. True love emanates out of the character of God. As I searched the street life for love, I always came up empty, and then God revealed to me that real love illuminates and it will not leave me in darkness.

Lord, I confess that I have not loved you as I should have. Father, you have been the only one who has seen me through every circumstance and you have given your all to me. Lord, I open my heart to you so that not only will you love me but I will love you in return. In Jesus' name, Amen.

Day 10

The Lord is at your right hand; he will crush kings on the day of his wrath.

Psalm 110:5

God will fight for us against our enemies, but He will fight according to His timing. Each battle is a testing ground for our faith and a time to call unto God to deliver us. Deliverance comes in many different ways and only God knows which will purify us and make Him to be glorified in all battles. But we have the assurance that, whichever way God chooses, it will make us stronger for His army. We should always be assured that the Commander of the Army is ever present with His warriors. God has strategically prepared us for battle if we would but follow the way He leads. The battle is designed not only for victory over our external enemies but also our internal ones. The internal battles can wage war longer than the external battles, and oftentimes internal victories will open up pathways for external ones. Allowing God to be ruler of my inner man gives me strength to overcome in my carnal exterior battles.

God, I see that I do not need deliverance in every battle but rather I need strength to go through it. Father Go, help me to trust in you and the strategies that you have planned in my battles that will allow me to be victorious through your power. In Jesus' name, Amen.

Father God, I understand now that true wisdom can and will only come when I am connected to you. Lord, I surrender to you that I may begin to know the way in which you want to lead me. In Jesus' name, Amen.

Day 11

The fear of the Lord is the beginning of wisdom;

Psalm 111:10

Until man respects who God is, he will always lack the ability to make sound decisions. We must come to a place where we lose ourselves in God, so that we may be found by Him. We will never understand all, but we need to respect God and give Him the honor for whatever decisions He wants to make, trusting that He knows best. Only then will enlightenment begin. Man has existed only using portions of our potential, but with God all abilities will be utilized. God seeks for us to be what He's designed, and He knows this is only possible by allowing Him to lead. Many times, as a Christian, I made my own decisions about life and did not consult God for true guidance and, as a result, I only tasted partial success. God wants us to live prosperously not have a little here and a little there. When we are living in true God prosperity, we have nothing missing, nothing lacking in any area of our lives.

Father God, I understand now that true wisdom can and will only come when I am connected to you. Lord, I surrender to you that I may begin to know the way in which you want to lead me. In Jesus' name, Amen.

Day 12

Blessed is the man who fears the Lord, who finds great delight in his commands.

Psalm 112:16

God blesses the man or woman who fears Him. In respecting God, He causes all areas of our lives to be blessed. God demands to have the top place in our mind, body, and soul. Every aspect of man God asks for keeps man in balance with His harmony of law and grace. When man delights in the things of God then God's peace will be upon that man. Whatever God asks us to do, it will be a joy to fulfill our Father's desire because what He is asking us for will bring pleasure to our lives. God has made it His business to satisfy man's every desire and by respecting God we shall live out this satisfied life designed for us.

God, I realize that things you ask me to do are for my own well-being. Lord, you only desire that I stay in harmony to your will. Father God, I am willing to accept your commands for my life. In Jesus' name, Amen.

Day 13

Let the name of the Lord be praised, both now and forever more.

Psalm 113:2

Praising the Lord and making sure His name is praised is more than just verbal praise. Praising God with our actions and how we handle situations is a real part of praise. The sanctuary isn't the only place for praise, but rather the common places we go. And it's not just always speaking the name of Jesus but speaking His name without saying a word. In every age of time God will have those who love Him so much that their lives will continue on the praise that began in Heaven. God's name is richer than just being printed on a page but His name is seen all around us in the existence of the world. God has blessed man with the privilege of praising His name but if man will not do the job then the elements will roar out the goodness of God. I was in jeopardy of allowing my praise to be stolen by rocks because I was living a life that brought praise to me instead of the one truly worthy to be praised. My choices brought me to a place where I had to dethrone myself and crown Jesus Lord and Savior of my life.

Lord God, teach me to praise you in every arena of life, so that it will draw people to you. Lord, now I see that my daily life that I live should sing of your praises. Father, forgive me for not praising you as I ought. In Jesus' name, Amen.

Day 14

Tremble, O earth, at the presence of the Lord, at the presence of the God Jacob.

Psalm 114:7

The presence of God breaks all yokes off of His children. This is where the believer longs to be. This is the place where transformation begins. This is a mandatory meeting place between God and man. The only way a Christian can continue to grow is in the presence of God. Impartation happens here. And this is the place where the Christian needs to dwell. God desires that we do more than just fall in and out of His presence; He wants His presence to be the headquarters of our entire decision making. When our thoughts are saturated with the presence of God then we are actually conveying His thoughts with our lives. There were times when I did not even know if God's presence was real, but when I tarried in prayer His presence was no longer a mystery. There are some things about God that will remain mysterious, but His presence should not be one. We have total access to God and should stop at nothing to get there so that we may dwell there for the entirety of our earthly existence.

Lord God, help me to get into your presence and dwell there. This is the place where I need to be. Lord, let nothing hinder me from getting to you. In Jesus' name, Amen.

Day 15

But their idols are silver and gold, made by the hands of men... The Lord remembers us and will bless us.

Psalm 115:4, 12

Because of man's desire to be glorified we miss out on the blessing to give God the praise. Often we set up gods in our lives that can give no deliverance but only aid in our rebellion. We are designed to give praise, yet we resist the designer of it. The only hope we have is in God; all of these false gods are in silence. God is looking to bless His people; God's people are looking in the wrong places for their blessings. Man chooses to give praise to the things we produce with our hands only to realize later that these things do not satisfy the true longing of the soul. While I was wasting time giving idol praise that only produced self-gratification, God was honoring His children who were giving Him true praise. God will honor and sustain the true worshippers of Him, and He will eternally silence all idol worshippers at His appointed time.

Father, I have been looking to the wrong gods. I have replaced you with false idol gods that cannot help or save me. Lord, help me to find my way back to you. Lord, I acknowledge you as the Only True God of the heavens and Earth. In Jesus' name, Amen.

Day 16

I was overcome by trouble and sorrow...Then I called on the name of the Lord: O Lord, save me.

(Ps.116:3-4).

Man has been operating under the authority that we can save ourselves. We live out this tragedy in the nations. Our view of who God has become distorted by our money, relationships, greed, anger, bitterness, drugs, food, and sex and so on; and the senses become numb to true salvation. Salvation is embodied in three phases: justification, sanctification and glorification. And during these phases a love, (AGAPE) for God develops and a hate for sin emerges. Many are lost because they have been their own savior for too long and yet they are still not saved. When relying on self for salvation, I found my troubles to be more than I was able to handle. As my own savior, I was hopeless and only found relief in vices that intoxicated my senses. Once I was down so low that all I could do was look up and call on the name of God; then restoration began in my life.

Heavenly Father, I have been trying to save myself for years only to realize that it cannot be done. Lord, I need you to take the place that is only designed for you. I accept you as my Lord and Savior. In Jesus' name, Amen.

Day 17

For great is His love towards us, and the faithfulness of the Lord endures forever.

(Ps.117:2)

Because of the purpose of God's love, we have not been consumed by sin. God cannot force His love upon us but even when our choices lead us to low places His love is evident in those places to rescue us. Not for the purpose man has used it for but allow us to repent from our old ways and walk in newness of life. God's love is what stays the hand of the enemy, and that same loving hand enforces discipline. Because we don't respect the Love of God, we abuse it but only to our detriment. God's love is what drives us to our purpose, which will bring glory to our marvelous Father. There were times in my life when I didn't know if love was real, but then I came into contact with the God who made love really exist. God's love is beyond good. His love sits on its own level. That's what makes it great. God did not just start loving this way; He has always loved this way. His faithfulness to the faithless is astounding.

Father, I have ignored your love for me and tried to use you for my own selfish gain. Father, I lack understanding about the purpose of your love for me and I need you to help me. Lord, I am tired of fighting against you. Lord help me. In Jesus' name.

Day 18

Give thanks to the Lord, for he is good: His love endures for ever.

Psalm 118:29

When we read that God's love endures forever, we must understand that there are no limitations on His love. God's love for us has discipline in it. Discipline is love. In His love He goes to every extreme to save our souls, and in His love He will let us go. The Bible says that the ones who fear God understand or are able to say His love endures forever. It is our privilege to give thanks to God for a never ending gift that He gives to us. God understands that when we truly are sincere about what we believe in, giving is automatic. If we know God to be good and believe in His goodness, then giving Him thanks is done without any prompting from man. When I was in the world, I believed that drugs would numb my pain, so I gave my money to get them. In the spirit, God does not numb pain. He heals pain and yet we act as though we must be begged to give God the thanks and praise that He deserves. If we don't give willfully now then God knows we will not give in heaven. Those who are looking forward to giving praise in Heaven are giving and living praise on Earth.

Father, what a sacrifice you have made for us to experience your love. God, open up my heart to so that it drinks up all that you have to give me. In Jesus' name, Amen.

Day 19

Blessed are they who keep his statues and seek him with all their heart.

Psalm 119:1 (Aleph 1-8)

God expects His children to walk in the ways that are His. We must search out the Word of God to find out what He wants. We like to use the excuse that we are humans and not perfect; however Christ himself was human but made choices that were pleasing to the Father. We want things to be our way, wanting to adopt the Word to fit our lives. We'd better make sure what we do is backed up by the Word of God. I often found myself doing things that pleased the world but grieved the Spirit, and the pleasures of the world are only temporal, so those euphoric feelings passed, leaving me empty again. God is saying, "Come drink from a well that shall never run dry," and we shall forever be watered by the Holy Spirit as we follow God's way.

Dear God, I know that your ways are not hard when I stay connected to you. I will only have peace when I follow after you, my God, Lord I am willing to do as you say; Father please teach me how. In Jesus' name, Amen.

Day 20

I will delight myself in thy statues: I will not forget thy word.

Psalm 119:16 (Beth 9-16)

Obeying a word or instruction helps the path that we walk become cleansed from willing disobedience. The world operates on instructions, it's all around us. People are either building their lives around a word from God or a word from the devil. Words are the frames to the houses we build. Obeying God's instructions, even if we don't understand them, give us an inner peace and respect for who He is. Out of this obedience springs up a well of joy for God and His will for our lives. Oftentimes we have followed our own guidance for so long that to obey God brings a war between the flesh and spirit. The scripture says, "I will" implying that even against my own self I must press my way into delighting in the way of my Lord. When I was saved it was a struggle to sit down and read the Word because I was so accustomed to running the streets but I had to force myself to stay in my home and read because I knew the desires of my flesh were only going to inflict further destruction on my life.

God, I see how powerful a word from you can be if I obey. I know not how to get where you need me to be without listening to you. I submit my will unto you, Father. Please save me, Lord, from myself. In Jesus' name, Amen.

Father God, give the true sight that I have been living without for so long. Holy Spirit, come into my life and illuminate what is living in darkness inside of me. In Jesus' name, Amen.

Day 21

Open thou mine eyes, that I may behold wondrous things out of thy law

Psalm 119:18 (Gimel 17-24)

To truly understand all that God speaks to us in His law, we must ask the Lord to give us true vision. God desires that we see beyond the natural; so He makes us dependant on Him for supernatural vision. Christ has to be invited in to abide, and his abiding brings illumination through the Holy Spirit. We shall never see into the unknown mysteries of God until the scales fall from our eyes and we can get that only from the Lord. When I think of the law through my natural eye I often think on something that limits me or prohibits me from doing what I want, but when I get revelation from God in my Spirit then I realize the law doesn't prohibit me; instead, it's an aid for me to experience the full benefits that God has for me.

Father God, give the true sight that I have been living without for so long. Holy Spirit, come into my life and illuminate what is living in darkness inside of me. In Jesus' name, Amen.

Day 22

I have chosen the way of truth: thy judgments have I laid before me.

Psalm 119:30 (Daleth 25-32)

When man continues in unrighteousness he develops a habit to sin. The only hope is to ask God to empower us to walk in His ways; which initially begins when we accept Christ as our Savior. Only then will we have enthusiasm, and a longing to follow a "Thus saith the Lord." The Lord will equip us to walk in His will, but it's our choice. Jesus does not only desire to be our Savior, He also wants us to be led by the Holy Ghost. These are choices that we must make on a daily basis in order to stay in the will of God. It is the freedom of our choice to get in His presence to receive daily directions. You never choose Jesus once and it settles it; Christ must be a constant choice we make on life's journey.

Heavenly Father, I thank you for the freedom of choice. It is a gift of awesome proportions. Lord, at this moment I choose your way and will for my life and I know, Lord, that you will give me all the tools to follow in your light. In Jesus' name, Amen.

Day 23

Stablish thy word unto thy servant, who is devoted to thy fear.

Psalm 119:38 (He 33-40)

If there is any true desire to succeed as a Christian, our dependency must be upon God. Every good and perfect gift comes from Him to those who are covered by the righteousness of Christ. God has not left any part of our life to our own discretion to lead on our own. He has supplied every need in order for us to be victorious in our fight against the devil. A daily encounter with God through praying, reading the Word, praise and worship will keep us from being only a hearer and make us also a doer for the Kingdom of God. We are in an era when self-reliance is becoming the common way of man. Positive thinking and,- letting go- of past hurts are good things to embrace, but these practices without true guidance and reliance on God may help us live a good life but not an eternal life. When God helped me to understand that there is a life after my earthly existence, I had to adjust my view on life to include eternity, and in that moment I realized that religion or religious acts would not do, I had to develop a relationship with God.

God, I realize that I must have an intimate encounter with you daily in order to be a true follower of yours. Lord, give me the strength to make that time with you. Father, I feel as though I am weak but, Lord, I am leaning on you as my source of strength. When I can't, I know you can. In Jesus' name, Amen.

Day 24

Let thy mercies come also unto me, O Lord, even thy salvation, according to thy word.

Psalm 119:41 (Vau 41-48)

God's word is true, infallible, empowering, enduring, rejuvenating, and just. What God has spoken will come to pass. The Lord expects those that believe on Him, to trust in Him. Faith is standing on every word that has come out of God's mouth. God justifies us, but in order to get from God what He wants for us we must ask, believe and claim His word and not waver. The currency of heaven is faith; faith will get a response from God every time. No matter how things may look in our lives when we hold by faith to what God has spoken we shall see heaven respond on our behalf. I am writing this from a jail cell and all around me looks hopeless, but when I look inside of me I see God. The vision of the eternal God living in me gives me faith to hold to His Word, and I shall see Him move.

God, I admit that I don't know your will because I have not been in your Word. You only have the words to life and eternal life. Lord, give me an appetite to study more so that I may know for sure the way you have predestined for me and by faith I will hold on to your every promise. In Jesus' name, Amen.

Day 25

This is my comfort in my affliction: for thy word hath quickened me.

Psalm 119:50 (Zain 49-56)

Pain is a teacher. Pain is designed to hurt so that we can grow. Whatever situation we may go through, God's Word can comfort us during those times to help us endure until the victory is released. Often in these times we turn to our own vices and at the end of our abuse we are no better. But in every encounter we have with the Word of God it cuts and heals, until finally the person that God has purposed us to be comes forth. God's word sharpens us until we no longer desire temporal deliverance from our pain, but rather we are fixed on our eternal victory. When I allowed God to help me fix my eyes on the solution instead of just the problem I could better endure my trials, knowing that the best me was going to emerge from the rubble of my situations.

Lord, when I am hurting, your Word is the last place I look to for hope and healing. God, fix my eyes on you so that I may know what true comfort is. Lord, I know that your Word will speak into my pain; help me not to resist you. In Jesus' name, Amen.

Day 26

Thou art my portion, O Lord: I have said that I would keep thy words.

Psalm 119:57 (Cheth 57-64)

Not until we give God what's His will we ever be satisfied. We will exhaust all avenues and still be empty inside. God has designed us to desire Him, only God can prolong our lives and make them abundant. When we allow God to be our portion He will then magnify all that we receive. God's desire is to be first in our lives and He will not accept any other position. When we receive God as our portion we shall see that nothing is missing and every place where we have been fractured He shall heal. We have been created with a place inside of us that only God can fill, He will not allow anyone or anything to have that place inside of our hearts.

Lord, help me to make you my portion so that I may truly know what it is to be filled up, the things of this world only make me empty inside. Lord, I am tired of that loneliness inside me. Awaken my love for you. In Jesus' name, Amen.

Day 27

Before I was afflicted I went astray: but now have I kept thy word.

Psalm 119:67 (Teth 65-72)

Affliction brings out either the desire to surrender or bitterness to resist. Affliction is a training ground for the righteous. God said affliction is a must for the righteous. It's delusional to think that we don't need affliction to thrust us into a deeper walk with God. Faith arises out of the fire of affliction. Endurance is tested, hope is deferred, patience is challenged, self- control is agitated but all graces to overcome are available. Affliction has a purpose, but only those with illuminated eyes will find the advantage. The illuminated eye will discern that affliction is not to bring us harm but to help birth growth. It was when I had to bear up under affliction that I really came to a real place of trusting in God.

Lord, I thought that my affliction was punishment from you, not understanding that this furnace will develop my character. Lord, I have assurance that you will not put on me more than I am able to bear, so continue to empower me to stand for you in affliction. In Jesus' name, Amen.

Day 28

Thy hands have made me and fashioned me: give me understanding, that I may learn thy commandments.

Psalm 119:73 (Jod 73-80)

God did more than just shape our physical exterior. He was not merely concerned with mankind looking like Him, but also with the inner man developing a love for Him. God had to stamp His sign on His creation, because He knew that man can alter the outer appearance. God knew that man could come to a place to have a form of godliness; He knew we could disguise our true spiritual state from the natural eye of man. But to change the inside of man only God can do that, without tearing the skin of man yet tearing the flesh. Until we understand that, we will only exist as a physical body. I realized that God had fashioned me for more than just to exist exteriorly; His truest desire was to bear the invisible Kingdom in my inner woman. When my Spirit woman begins to enlarge then the mysteries of God will be revealed.

Lord, I know that you desire an inner change for me and only you can do that in me. Lord, I see that outer beauty without inner beauty is only vanity. Father, help me to focus on becoming more like you in my inner man. In Jesus' name, Amen.

Day 29

Quicken me after thy loving kindness; so shall I keep the testimony of thy mouth.

Psalm 119:88 (Caph 81-88)

To be quickened after the loving kindness of God makes the spirit of man respond to love. When encountered with love, an inner joy rushes through the being. Man will long to be in contact with those who the love of God permeates from. The fashioning process that God did for man was instilling us with the capacity to love. In the days that we live in, God is taking us back to primitive godliness, and love is the bond that sets us apart from the devil and his angels. When I tasted of God's real love, a decoy could no longer keep me bound, and it could no longer satisfy the true longing of my spirit. The Spirit of God began to make me aware of the false love and would guide me away from indulging in false love that will only last for a season.

God, help me to love people as you have loved me. Lord, let your love quicken me from a selfish love into a selfless love. In Jesus' name, Amen.

Day 30

Forever, O Lord, thy word is settled in heaven.

Psalm 119:89 (La-med 89-96)

All good things come to an end; that's what we have been taught. But these so called good things are the pleasures of this world. God has intended for us to have joy in this world through His will for us. We want to take perversion, lust, lying, drugs, manipulation and so on and call these things good. These things are good only at deceiving people into believing that some form of goodness comes from them. Everything that exists as good has to come from God. He is the author of good and there is none else. The settling of God's Word can never be uprooted, but the pleasures of this world continue to show us on a daily basis that they have an expiration date. For some of us reading this it was revealed through jail, pregnancies, addictions, losing our families' support, children, etc. There is only one author whose words shall always remain and that author is God. So whatever God has spoken about your life will come to pass; so we must allow the pure Word of God to uproot all the lies planted within us from this world.

Lord, I have been disillusioned by thinking that worldly pleasures bring goodness. Lord, help me to find my joy in being with you and living life through your Word. In Jesus' name, Amen.

God, your words have sweetness like nothing else. Give me a taste that will desire more of what you say. Lord, let the sweetness of your words change the sourness of my spirit. In Jesus' name, Amen.

Day 31

How sweet are thy words unto my taste! Yea sweeter than honey to my mouth.

Psalm 119:103 (Mem 97-104)

Finding love in the law of God means loving what God says about Himself and man. The law teaches us how to love the Creator and His creation. Following what God has taught us is only difficult when we are secretly rebelling against Him. Once we make a commitment to do as God asks us and no matter what we stand on that vow, God will empower us to obey Him through love. Only then what God says to us will be sweet. Once we taste of God's Word, nothing will ever satisfy that taste except God's Word. We cannot just attempt to do the works of righteousness but have no connection to the Righteousness one. The deeper we develop a love affair with God the sweeter His words become to our souls. Once I submitted to God's leading, His words began to penetrate into places inside of me that were dry and bitter and then healing began. I found it impossible to continuously be washed in God's sweetness and remain bitter; His sweetness changed my bitter into better.

God, your words have sweetness like nothing else. Give me a taste that will desire more of what you say. Lord, let the sweetness of your words change the sourness of my spirit. In Jesus' name, Amen.

Day 32

Thy word is a lamp unto my feet, and a light unto my path.

Psalm 119:105 (Nun 105-112)

The Word of God has a double illumination. The Word illuminates our interior and exterior. The mind is sharpened and the eyes are opened. When we are walking in darkness our decisions are all made in the dark. Only light makes things seen and brings forth repentance for bad decisions we have made. We will never grasp what God has in store for us until He brings His light to us, and we accept. Light never disappears, darkness tries to cover it, but true enlightenment knows that darkness is only a trial period for growth in Christ. That light comes in the person of Jesus Christ. We must accept Him for the illumination process to begin. I can remember times doing drugs and saying that it helped me to focus or think clearer but that clear thinking never birthed anything productive in me. Sometimes we can be walking in artificial light yet thinking it is true light, but the test is to see if this light has birthed positive changes in our lives. Jesus the true Light illuminates so that we can see to live better, and if the light we have is not doing that then we are not yet connected to the True Light.

Lord, I have been living in darkness so long that I didn't realize that I couldn't see. Father, I accept the true light through Jesus Christ my Lord and Savior. Allow me to see as you have designed me to. In Jesus' name, Amen.

Day 33

I hate vain thoughts: but thy law do I love.

Psalm 119:113 (Sa-mech)

The devil understands that, if mankind becomes mentally connected to Christ, He will lose many souls. When a Christian is linked with God mentally then those mental pictures coming from God will come out of the Christian's mouth and take dominion as God has ordained. So Satan will tempt us to dwell on vain thoughts, empty thoughts, and self- motivated thoughts then all that comes from our mouths will war with God's will. There has to be a balance within the Christian to love God and all His ways and to hate the devil and all his ways. When the mind is focused on Christ, then He will empower us to live as we ought to live as His followers. As we allow God to break us, the hardest thing to let go of is our mental strongholds because we are under a false sense of control. Only when we allow God to break those strongholds, that traditional thought process, will we see God at work in us and through us in limitless ways.

Lord, I have been professing you with my mouth, but with my mind I have been serving the devil. Father, help me to surrender to you totally so that no part of me will I withhold from you. God, break the mental chains that I am bound to; that I may know true freedom. In Jesus' name, Amen.

Day 34

I am thy servant; give me understanding, that I may know thy testimonies.

Psalm 119:125 (Ain 121-128)

Once we accept the adoption into the family of God, our Father becomes responsible for giving us our gifts. Adoption is really an empowerment experience to the inner man. Now mankind has the right to accept and receive the promises that are in God's word, and see them fulfilled. Mankind will also have a better understanding of which he belongs to. God gives us the power to speak into existence what is the will of God for our lives. The profession from man is backed up with the provision that God has already supplied for the need. When the enemy had me in error of who I was then I was in a constant yearning of not knowing who I was, but when the Lord opened my understanding to who I really was and that I was created on purpose, my life began to come together likes puzzle pieces and God was the glue.

God, I am thankful that I can call you Father. Lord, help me to understand whose family I represent every day. I see that promises are for your children and you fulfill every promise that you have spoken. Help me to obey you, Daddy, that I bring glory to your name. In Jesus' name, Amen.

Day 35

The entrance of thy words giveth light; it giveth understanding unto the simple.

Psalm 119:130 (Pe 129-136)

    A word from the mouth of God brings order to any situation going on in my life. It's not just speaking a word that puts them into action but the belief in what has been spoken not only belief in what's said but in who is saying it. Jesus gave us this example as He walked the earth as a human who believed in God. We will never receive the fruits of the Word of God until we believe beyond the natural. When I walked away from the drug life, I was walking on the power of words spoken by God. He said the best life for me was in Him, so I stepped out on that Word and I have not looked back in fifteen years. I found out on my journey that, even if the situation did not change, God had done a work in me so that I became the change I desired to see. Will all things work out the way we want? Emphatically, " No"!" But a word from God will keep me focused even when I don't see what I want.

Lord, you have spoken words that can change my situation, help me to believe in them. Lord, help me to get closer to you so that I will be empowered by your words. In Jesus' name, Amen.

Day 36

The righteousness of thy testimonies is everlasting, give me understanding, and I shall live.

Psalm 119:144 (Tzad-di 137-144)

There will never exist a time when God is not righteous. The righteousness of mankind is not based upon our abilities to make us righteous but solely on the righteousness of Jesus Christ alone. Every reward that we experience in the existence of time is a result of the timeless righteousness of God. As we see God clothed in His righteousness, that He gave us through Jesus, we shall understand why God does what He does for us. Man can't explain it, but the true believer accepts it and walks in His righteousness. Every good thing that flows into our lives is a result of Jesus' righteousness and not ours, but His righteousness affords us all the benefits of heaven. Understanding righteousness by faith was hard for me to grasp because my mindset of receiving it was based upon the works of my hands. Coming to the place to understand God's incredible gift to me took me many years to really flow in this place, but I realized anything less would make Jesus' sacrifice null and void. We must receive this gift by faith to truly walk in the Kingdom of God.

Lord, I have no way of doing right without your righteousness in my life. God, I will ever do wrong if you do not lead me. Father, please be my guide because I know not the way to go. In Jesus' name, Amen.

Day 37

I cried with my whole heart; hear me, O Lord: I will keep thy statues.

Psalm 119:145 (Koph 145-152)

There are moments on this Christian journey where we must be broken, and during this process the mentality is strained and the spirit is tested. Tears become an un-welcomed visitor, and sleep can become a stranger. This is the time in which God is calling us higher, and fear can remind us that we are off the ground. But family we must close our eyes, open our hearts and remember that we can fly. The Law of Gravity does not apply in our spirit. Brokenness births elevation in the spirit realm, and often this is the only place where we fit in now. Every human emotion must bow to the trust we now have in God. Sometimes we want to avoid brokenness but I am a witness that it can birth great hope not only for self but others as well.

Dear God, my heart is heavy with pain because I have allowed fear to take over. Lord, free me from this bondage that I am in. Lord, save me from the demon of fear. In Jesus' name, Amen.

Day 38

I beheld the transgressors, and was grieved; because they kept not thy word.

Psalm 119:158 (Resh 153-160)

When there is hate for sin, there should be a compassion for sinners. No matter how many acts of violence, abuse of drugs, or neglect of children is seen there should be grief in the soul of the Christian. To watch God's children search the world to fill His place should take the intercessors to the threshing floor. God should hear harmonious cries coming from Earth for the salvation of mankind. As believers we should never stop pleading the blood to change the lives of those who are lost, or for those who are lost but think they are saved. We must be mindful that we too were once estranged from God and by His grace He wooed us to His side and now we have the opportunity to help others be reconciled to Him.

Dear God, save me so that I may help my brothers and sisters who are lost. God, help us to see that it is not your will for us to be lost. Lord, use me as your hands and your feet to offer salvation to man. In Jesus' name, Amen.

Day 39

Seven times a day do I praise thee because of thy righteous judgments.

Psalm 119:164 (Schin 161-168)

God is seeking for us to praise Him to perfection. That does not mean that we are without flaws, rather it means that we are not practicing sinning. Perfecting our praise has more to do with us maturing and living a life of worship. Whenever the Spirit of God moves upon us to show forth praise, we must simply obey Him. Obedience is the key to perfecting praise. God is not comparing our praises; He just wants the best from each of us individually. Perfect praise is birthed out of the gratitude the believer has towards God's righteousness. Perfect praise takes all attention, glory, and accolades away from man and is expressed to God who is righteous. I find that the perfection of praise lifts us into a place of worship and in that intimate place with God man disappears and God's presence is revealed.

Father God, I know that I don't give you the praise that you so rightly deserve. Lord, show me how to pour out of my spirit all the praise that you are calling forth from my life. Let me not hold back what permeates the very atmosphere of heaven, which is, untiring praise. In Jesus' name, Amen.

Day 40

My tongue shall speak of thy word; for all thy commandments are righteousness.

Psalm 119:172 (Tan 169-176)

God has given man many gifts and the tongue is one of them. God designed that we would submit our members unto Him, making the whole body subject to Him. Because of our inclination to sin we must force our members to do His will. He has graced our tongues to pack the power of creation in them; they're like nuclear weapons, so we must be careful with what we say. They are designed to bring life to people by speaking God's Word to them. The tongue has a purpose in building the Kingdom of God and it must be used for His glory; anything other than that will result in condemnation to self and man. The greatest revelation that I got from what was coming from my tongue was that I spoke what I put in me. My words reflected my thoughts; so in order for my words to change I had to change what I was thinking on.

Dear God, I have taken your gift and used it for my own pleasure. Lord, I have spoken things that have brought dishonor to the Giver of the gift. Father, help me to open my mouth for your glory and not to lend my instruments to unrighteousness. In Jesus' name, Amen.

Lord, help me to just stop asking you to deliver me out of trouble instead of asking for strength to go through. God, I need to be more like you, please continue to shape me using the methods that you see are necessary. In Jesus' name, Amen.

Day 41

In my distress I cried unto the Lord, and he heard me.

Psalm 120:1

Distressed situations always send out a distress signal. In the natural realm the common one is S.O. S., which means get me out of trouble. In the spiritual realm it is "Jesus, help," which translates in our minds as, "Get me out of this situation right now." There are times in the spirit realm when we get our distress signals confused with the natural. Jesus wants more than to deliver us from temporal problems; He desires to change our minds toward sin. A true distress call is deeper than "Get me out of trouble," but rather it's, "Lord, change me so that I won't continue on this path." Even if God doesn't remove us from our trouble that doesn't mean that He hasn't heard and answered our call for help. Once the call has left our mouth, God assesses it and responds according to what we need to draw us closer to Him. There were many times when I sent a distress call out to God and wanted instant deliverance but that was not what I needed. God knows what we really need in our distressed situations, and we must trust His response.

Lord, help me to just stop asking you to deliver me out of trouble instead of asking for strength to go through. God, I need to be more like you, please continue to shape me using the methods that you see are necessary. In Jesus' name, Amen.

Day 42

The Lord shall preserve thy going out and thy coming in from this time forth and even for evermore.

Psalm 121:8

Once you come into a relationship with God, He is responsible for keeping you in all that you do for building the Kingdom. As long as we continue to walk in His way, God will be a shield of defense to His people. The only way that God's protection is not felt in our lives is a result of our disobedience. Every place in life that we enter into or come out of, God's preserving power will be felt. The moment that we come into covenant with God, He keeps us and continues because He is Faithful to Himself and His word. This does not mean that I now can live however I want because He is covering me rather it shows me the depth of His love to save me and that brings about a great change in my heart to not want to live without God. God still has things that He has spoken that He must keep, grace is one and judgment is another. The same God who loved me enough to cover me will be the same loving God who will render a fair judgment upon me.

Father God, I have wandered outside of your provision for me and I have disobeyed you. Lord, I know that I cannot make it without you; please illuminate the way so that I can see which way you want me to go. In Jesus' name, Amen.

Day 43

For there are set thrones of judgment, the thrones of the house of David.

Psalm 122:5

None will be able to escape judgment. There is coming a time when we all will have to answer for our choices, and then we will stand before God's judgment seat. Oftentimes the thought of judgment is not convincing enough for us to change our ways. Judgment is deeper than doing away with the bad it is a revelation of the love that God has for mankind. The Lord longs for the day when He can be with His people, so He awaits judgment Himself. The Lord desires that we all be saved; this is why His mercy is still pleading with man. God is looking forward to a loving future with mankind and only judgment will usher this in. Mankind lives under the delusion that we can live any way we want and somehow still be saved; this is an example of those who have fallen in love with the world. The moment is now to repent, at judgment it will be too late. Judgment will be the beginning of an eternal love affair we will begin with God uninterrupted.

Lord, I am not ready to stand before you in judgment. Heavenly Father, please help me to accept your gift of salvation. Lord, I feel as though I have messed my chances up but, Lord, I am hoping in your Word to be saved. In Jesus' name, Amen.

Day 44

Our soul is exceedingly filled with the scorning of those that are at ease, and with the contempt of the proud.

Psalm 123:4

The believer must keep their eyes focused on Christ, or the distractions of the world will frustrate them. It may seem as if the sinner continues on his journey with ease while the Christian struggles. The sinner may gain temporal things but at the cost of the spirit being lost. A fixed eye on Christ will birth inside of the Christian the understanding that every need is met and confidence shall arise as God manifests His miracles in the lives of His children. The world must see the Christian struggle so that they get a glimpse of faith under fire. God has promised that in every struggle we will come out victorious. Spiritual inheritance far outweighs temporal gain that doesn't glorify Christ. I could understand incarceration while I sold drugs but to be hit with a petty family dispute that caused me, as a Christian, to be locked up blew my mind. God gave me but a few moments to make the choice to trust Him even in this and as I wiped my face and said, "Yes Lord," it all became so clear that this was not just about me but so that God could shine His light through me to bring weary travelers home to Him.

God, I think at times that the wicked are more prosperous than Christians and it angers me. Lord, give me your eyes so that I may see as you. Help me not to sacrifice my relationship with you for temporal prosperity. In Jesus' name, Amen.

Day 45

They that trust in the Lord shall be as mount Zion which cannot be removed, but abideth forever.

Psalm 125:1

Trust is an anchor for the soul. What you trust in determines your destiny. Trust in the Lord makes the believer unmovable. Trust grows roots in the believer toward the Word of God, which is God's character. Once we come into a relationship with God, His word is what sustains us. When we truly let the Word of God abide in us through trust we shall live forever in the presence of God. He empowers us through trust to stand against the works of the enemy. Trust has to be more than something we say; it has to be embedded in all our actions. Trust is a communicative word; so when confronted by the devil he can discern if our trust in God is truly real. Trust in God proves to God that we believe who He is without seeing first what He can do.

Lord, I admit that I trust you with my emotions rather than the principle that you are trust. Father, I know that I doubt your ways and so I ask for forgiveness. God, help me to trust even when I can't see the outcome. In Jesus' name, Amen.

Day 46

He that goeth forth and weepeth, bearing precious seed, shall doubtless come again with rejoicing, bringing his sheaves with him.

Psalm 126:6

Being a sower of the Word of God brings some sorrow with the calling. The Word of God is a double edged sword, so before healing comes, a cutting must happen. The Word exposes the truth to the sower, so nothing is hid. Sowers experience the pain of transgression in their lives and in the lives of those around them. When one becomes a true sower of the Word, sensitivity arises in one's heart to his and her fellow brethren. And even amidst the pain that is brought, joy still arises as some souls are saved. As sowers, God gives us insights into His pain and joy that He experiences while dealing with sin yet loving the sinner. Bearing the Word of God comes with a price, and it also comes with rewards. This scripture reminded me in my dark hours that it would not be dark always, and there is a set time when rejoicing will arise again out of my tear stained voice.

Dear Lord, I hurt as I see your people struggle with the enemy and lose. God, it feels as though my labor is in vain, but, God I know that I am not in control. Father, I need you to save your people from the traps of the enemy. Lord, let me be faithful in sowing your Word. In Jesus' name, Amen.

Day 47

Lo, children are an heritage of the Lord: and the fruit of the womb is his reward.

Psalm 127:3

Though parents want their children to be the spoil of their life; the truth is they are God's reward. God has designed that the children of the earth be His inheritance. As joint heirs with Christ, the children are to represent the Kingdom they belong to. We have allowed our children to become false heirs of the earth, and so they desire no true relationship with God during their youth. We have fed them with the pleasures of this world, so they have no taste for heavenly things. The training of God's reward begins for the child in the womb. Before conception parents should saturate the womb with the presence of God. Children will be taught more by the way they see their parents live, so that should make parents mindful of how they live before their children. What God claims as a reward He will collect on; and when parents stand before God, they will have to give an account to Him about the children He lent them.

Father God, I have not treasured the gift you have loaned to me. Lord, I have misrepresented your character to your children. God, forgive me for not investing in them as you would have me do. Lord, train me in your ways so that I may train your children. **In Jesus' name, Amen.**

Day 48

Blessed is everyone that feareth the Lord; that walketh in his ways.

Psalm 128:1

God's Word has no respect of persons, His promises stand for anyone who has accepted Jesus as their personal Savior. Man gets discouraged by the outward appearance but God is working on the heart of man. God knows that it is an easy thing for us to clean up outwardly and yet the inside be dirty. God has spoken His word and it stands forever. His promises are fulfilled prophesies that He has spoken. God understands what we need to stand against the enemy, so He gave us the most powerful weapons in the heavenly arsenal. The Lord has instructed us that as we have reverence and respect towards Him, blessings shall be upon us. There is no way we will not be blessed if we do as God instructed. I found that the state of being blessed had to become my thought process so that, no matter what came up against me, I still knew I was blessed. Blessed is not about things but it is an innermost peace that I am in harmony with God, and when we are in line with God then all things shall line up.

Father God, I have been walking in the path that I wanted. Lord, I have taken no regard for your council, nor have I feared you. God, make me a new person who will obey what you say, and enjoy every command that you speak. In Jesus' name, Amen.

Day 49

Many a time have they afflicted me from my youth; yet they have not prevailed against me.

Psalm 129:2

There are some of God's children who feel as though they have been living in the furnace of affliction. At every season of life it seems as if affliction is your portion. If affliction seems to be your cup then focusing on the product of affliction, rather than the flames of affliction will strengthen you. Affliction is designed to bring forth a vessel for God's glorification. There are lessons in our lives we will only learn through affliction. Only those whom God truly loves does He chasten. As we overcome every afflicting trial we see clearer the power of God to bring us through. Affliction brings us to a place where we cry out for God's help, and we rely on Him leading us. We have allowed so many things to substitute God in our lives that He must remind us of whom He is. Even in affliction God has weighed it out so that it will not overtake us. He still takes most of the blows in our trials and tribulations. Affliction is the tool that God allows to train, shape, and mold His followers. I often found myself praying for God to deliver me from afflictions rather than strength to go through them and when God did not answer my request I would shut down on Him, but as I grew in the Lord the Holy Spirit taught me the value of afflictions and how something much greater in my character was being worked out through affliction. Afflictions may not be welcomed but they do a work that nothing else can do and that often draws us closer to God and to a place of total surrender.

God, I feel like I am crying out to you every day and you don't hear me. Lord, I feel as though I am going to break while going through this trial. Father, strengthen me to go through so that I may get out of this trial what you have designed for me to have. In Jesus' name, Amen.

Day 50

But there is forgiveness with thee, that thou mayest be feared.

Psalm 130:4

Forgiveness is a gift that God gives us to display His love for us. In every relationship there are expectations and with God it's not any different. He gives all that He can give to us in hopes that we will give our all to Him. God's character is revealed to us so that we may revere who He is. We are eternally indebted to Him for all of the wonderful things He has done to make mankind the dominant species upon this earth. True forgiveness in humanity is a supernatural gift. When man truly has a relationship with the Lord

God, you will see it in his willingness to forgive one another. Forgiveness is a two way path; it goes backwards and heals the offender and forward to heal the offended. To forgive a person who may have offended you will open your mental prison doors and to be forgiven by a victim of your offence removes their shackles. Forgiveness is a gift of freedom, sow it generously and receive it generously.

Lord, I have been holding things against people and I can't seem to forgive them and there are people who are hurting because of my offense to them. God, I understand that if I won't forgive then you won't forgive. Father, I need to move on and let these people free from my secret bondage. Help me, Lord, to forgive them and to be forgiven. In Jesus' name, Amen.

Day 51

Lord, my heart is not haughty, nor mine eyes lofty: neither do I exercise myself in great matters, or in things too high for me.

Psalm 131:1

The Lord does not save us so that we can think more of ourselves than we ought. God does not want to bring us out of some things in our lives so that we begin to praise and glorify ourselves. True salvation glorifies the giver of the gift not the receiver. God made salvation an unconditionally free gift so that man couldn't take any credit; hence, there should not arise a desire to be praised. God has made our journeys individually different to bring out Him in us. The Lord is looking to see His Son in our actions, in our hearts, and our treatment of mankind. All good gifts working through us are flowing out of the goodness of God and it is our responsibility, as believers, to always acknowledge that to those who are giving the gift. We have a great opportunity to guide people to God when we give Him back the glory for the good they see in us.

Dear God, I have exalted my ways and thoughts over yours. I have been claiming glory for what you only have done. Lord, take these foolish ways and thoughts out of mind, so that I may give all the glory and honor to you. Father, You alone deserve the praise; forgive me for stealing from you. In Jesus' name, Amen.

Day 52

I will not give sleep to mine eyes, or slumber to mine eyelids, until I find out a place for the Lord, an habitation for the mighty God of Jacob.

Psalm 132:4, 5

To what extreme will we go to seek out God and prepare our place for Him to dwell in us? What are we willing to give up for His habitation within us, or what are we willing to hold on to that will keep Him at bay? To allow God to live in us we must be willing to make sacrifices. When God moves inside of us there are things that will automatically come out. God's dwelling place will level the ground that we are standing on in order for Him to elevate us to where He is. There is a clearing of our ground, internally, that must happen for the Lord to be and do all that He wants for us. When God dwells in us, He's looking for a vessel that He can bless, which will bless His people. God dwelling in man is not for a selfish agenda but rather so God can use the dweller to bring people to Him. Ultimately, as Christians, that's what we should be seeking.

Father God, I have made my temple a dwelling place for everyone and everything but you. Lord, I have taken the very sanctuary that you gave to me and kicked you out of it. God, have mercy upon me for my foolish ways. Lord, give me the strength to make you the head of this home. In Jesus' name, Amen.

Day 53

Behold, how good and how pleasant it is for brethren to dwell together in unity!

Psalm 133:1

Unity among God's people carries a commanded blessing with it. True unity only happens when mankind surrenders our will to the will of God. Man in him or herself can't unify on anything without the Lord making the moves in them. In God's unity there is no personal self agenda that is exalted. This is the form in which God is glorified, His presence felt, and His character manifested. Unity draws people to God because He is the head of unity. Unity among God's children makes His presence felt and experienced when they gather together. The church becomes a movement when unity is found in the congregation of the brethren. Many times we have allowed disagreements make us disagreeable. I truly believe the devil uses this to cripple the church from coming together to make a Kingdom impact upon this dark world. Jesus Christ should be the focus of our unity and when He is it equips us in all arenas of life to bring His presence to the people.

Lord, if I am not unified with you how can I be unified with your people? Father, please help me to stop trying to control you. Lord, we are at odds because I have not surrendered to your will. God, help me to let go so you can release your power in my life. In Jesus' name, Amen!

Day 54

The Lord that made heaven and earth bless thee out of Zion.

Psalm 134:3

The blessings that God has in store for mankind are not derived from the earth. Blessings come from a place of purity and supernatural power. God's blessings are limitless, while Satan's counterfeits come from a shallow reservoir. Because blessings are of a supernatural proportion they are not designed just for the receiver to hoard. God blesses His people so that it can be a witness to those who don't know Him correctly. The same creative power that God used to create the world is the same power in which the blessing of God rests upon the believer. The blessing is meant to overpower the thwarts of the devil, and to warn the enemy that this soul has entered into the Blood Covenant with God. Where the blessing is found, the Lord is abiding. Divine blessings from God will always reveal their substance based upon eternal principles because God is not blessing just for earthly purposes. Our greatest blessing will not be temporal but eternal, so beware of the decoy blessings that the enemy will try to trap us in.

Lord, I have no true understanding of what it means to have your blessing in my life. I have been thinking that the blessing meant stuff and, Lord, I am so wrong. Father, teach more about what the blessing really is so that I may teach others. In Jesus' name, Amen.

Day 55

Ye that stand in the house of the Lord, in the courts of the house of our God.

Psalm 135:2

      Each opportunity and blessing that we have to stand in God's courts is an honor from God. When the Lord grants us to come into His presence in His house, we should sing forth with praise and exaltation. God's house of worship has become a routine stop during the week, so the praise and worship is minimal. God's house is no longer sacred to us; it is no longer a sanctuary. When the time comes for us to assemble to worship God corporately, we no longer have the desire to be there with Him. If there is any form of struggle, physically or mentally, we will give in to those emotions and skip yet another opportunity to give back to God. It matters not what the temple may look like; it only matters that God meets with His people there. He counts it a loss when we don't show up to love on Him in worship as a body. Many times, when I was at my weakest moments, it was when I went to the House of God and heard others worshipping that I gained strength, focus and hope to go on. Don't allow the enemy to block an opportunity to be filled by the Holy Spirit- even if you don't "feel' like it, press on anyway.

Dear God, I have not valued being in your house of worship. Lord, I have treated your sanctuary as a common place. Father, revive a new spirit in me so that I may understand the price you paid for me to be in your house. In Jesus' name, Amen.

Day 56

O give that unto the God of heaven: for his mercy endureth for ever.

Psalm 136:26

There is only one reason why the devil has not been able to overcome us, and that is because of God's enduring mercy. God has every right to allow suffering to come upon us and have its way, but His mercy for us says no. There are attributes of the character of God that are simply unexplainable and mercy is one of them. God's mercy has spanned generation after generation and it will continue to go on because it is His desire. Mercy has nothing to do with man earning it; it is a gift God gives in whatever circumstance and degree that He wants to express it. Once mankind receives Christ as Savior, and allows Him to operate as Lord, mercy is greatly appreciated by the newborn man. God's gifts have no expiration date on them; so as long as man operates in God then the resources are bountiful. God's mercy in mankind helps to see the heart of man, instead of the outward display. Mercy has spiritual insight built into it, so man won't be quick to judge by first glance at a person and their situation. God allows mercy to flow freely; so man should give without reserve. All of mankind has received mercy, which is a gift from God that we did not deserve.

Heavenly Father, I thank you for your mercy. Lord, I have not even realized how it has kept me alive. Lord, help me not to be dull to the diversity of your character. God, teach me to freely give your gift to man as you endlessly have given to me. In Jesus' name, Amen.

Day 57

How shall we sing the Lord's song in a strange land?

Psalm 137:4

Sometimes we arrive at place in our lives and because the situation looks hopeless, we begin rebelling against God. God has allowed His people to enter strange lands not because of His anger but rather because of His grace and mercy. When things are going smoothly for us, we can sing God's praises with each note going higher and higher. But when times arise and everything around is unfamiliar and rocky, we seem to forget our song and even the tune in which His praises are sung. Our truest song will always be sung in a place that we are being pressed in. In this strange land where it seems nothing good can come from it the most beautiful piece you will sing will arise out of your belly. There is no better way to find uncharted territory. For at this place you will see the result of true praise and worship. For many years I was singing a song of comfort and it was not until I got into a place of pressing that I learned how to truly worship God in spite of, and regardless of, my situation or circumstances.

Dear God, may I have the strength to sing a song to you in every season. In times past I have allowed trials and tribulations to steal my song for you. Lord, give me endurance in these times so that I may continue to sing your praises. In Jesus' name, Amen.

Day 58

The Lord will perfect that which concerneth me: thy mercy, O Lord, endureth for ever: forsake not the works at thine own hands.

Psalm 138:8

Perfection only happens by the hands of God. There is nothing that man can do to perfect His ways, all perfection comes from God. God knows us better than we will ever know ourselves, so He is in tune with our weaknesses and what to do to strengthen them. God's perfecting does not look like man's because God is perfecting them from the inside out. He is committed to making us perfect in His sight and not the sight of man. As we walk with God we will realize that man's perfection doesn't measure up to God's. Man's system is flawed and will never shape us into a perfect vessel. It is not the absence of flaws that makes us perfect; it is the absence of self. When I let go of the external perfecting system of man and embraced the internal system of God then I positioned myself to become all God has designed me to be.

Dear God, I have no chance of making myself perfect. This is a process that only you can do. Lord, I know now that the perfection you want is not the way man thinks it is. Father, perfect me in the ways that please you so that I may reflect you. In Jesus' name, Amen.

Day 59

Though I walk in the midst of trouble, thou wilt revive me: thou shalt stretch forth thine hand against the wrath of mine enemies, and thy right hand shall save me.

Psalm 138:7

When we are going through times of trouble it can seem as if the very life is being sucked out of us. Trouble sends a transmission to the body in the message of fatigue. We get drained during these times because we are not drawing from the source of life. Only the Word of God can sustain us during these seasons, but instead of us continuing to feed on God through study and prayer, we starve our spirit by our disconnection. If we stay in union with God, He will restore what energy we have lost and stretch His hand out against our enemies. We forget in these situations that we still have the authority through Christ surging through us, and all we need say is, "Peace Be Still." Trials and tribulations overtake us because we have become fatigued in the power of God. Trouble often led me to ask for the Holy Spirit's presence like never before because all my natural abilities and knowledge became useless. I know now that without the Holy Spirit keeping me supernaturally connected, trouble would overtake me. In trouble and out of trouble, ask the Holy Spirit to fill you.

Lord God, though I have lacked faith during this trial I am asking you to renew my Spirit. God, forgive me for my doubting and for not nourishing our marriage during this time. Lord, I have a blood bought right to your power and I speak to be overtaken with that power right now in the name of Jesus. Amen.

DAY 60

For there is not a word in my tongue, but, lo, O Lord, thou knowest it altogether.

Psalm 139:4

God is so acquainted with us that before we speak a word; He already knows what we are going to say. It would seem that He has as advantage over us but the fact is if we became acquainted with God's Word then we would know His will for our lives. During seasons of trial, we become rash with our tongues because the time needed in God's Word has been forfeited. Every time we miss an opportunity to be in the presence of God, His ways become more unknown to us, although we are never unknown to Him. When we spend time in the Word of God, in His Presence, and flowing in the Holy Spirit, it takes away some of the mystery that shrouds God's character. In that time, He is not seen as a distant God but rather a close Father. I was amazed at how God knew me and saw me in my weakest and ugliest moments, but He still wanted a relationship with me. I was estranged from God and yet here I sit in a deeper relationship with Him, and if that can happen to me then, rest assured, it can happen for you.

Lord, I come to you to ask for forgiveness because I have become unknown to your will for my life through neglect of spending quality time with you. Father, extinguish the fire that my tongue has caused in my life. Lord, I surrender my will so I may know your will for my life. I thank you, Lord, for all I must do is ask according to your Word. In Jesus' name Amen.

www.ingramcontent.com/pod-product-compliance
Lightning Source LLC
Chambersburg PA
CBHW042332150426
43194CB00001B/36